# Creation's Path

*A poetic journey of faith.*

Liza my Love
&

Sharon D. Holliday

Thanks

Sharon Holliday

# Creation's Path

*A poetic journey of faith.*

Sharon D. Holliday

ARMOUR OF LIGHT
PUBLISHING
Charleston, South Carolina · Chapel Hill, North Carolina

Published in the United States of America by
Beautiful Feat Press
*an imprint of*
Armour of Light Publishing
P.O. Box 778
Chapel Hill, North Carolina  27514

Visit us at: www.armouroflight.org

Design by Michael E. Evans

ISBN  978-0-9817120-1-7

LCCN  2008926305

First Edition

10 9 8 7 6 5 4 3 2 *1*

Unless otherwise indicated, Bible quotations are taken from New King James Version of the Bible by Thomas Nelson Publishers copyright 1990, 1985, 1983. Copyright © 1973, 1978, 1984 by International Bible Society at Zondervan.

New International Version (NIV)
Copyright © 1973, 1978, 1984 by International Bible Society

The Amplified Bible (AMP)
Copyright © 1954, 1958, 1962, 1964, 1965, 1987 by The Lockman Foundation.

# Acknowledgments

Sincere Thanks

To my loving husband, Minister Ransom D. Holliday,
Your love and support of my time and dedication to God to fulfill
my purpose does not go unnoticed. As we walk together to com-
plete our destiny, my heart rejoices because we share this journey. I
desire that you always experience the bountiful joy and the bless-
ings of God for all you do.  My sincere love and thankfulness.


Love and Thanks to my Mom, Esther Thomas,
on your knees you help me stand,
And Dad, James Moore--A father's love can carry you through the
toughest times and cause you to stand through it all.
You are wonderful parents.

To my children, I am blessed to have you, my love and thanks.


Special thanks to a wonderful son-in-law.
Quincey your invaluable support throughout this journey has
manifested new meaning to "being there."
My sincere love and thanks.
You are son, you are friend.


To my family and friends, you are truly a blessing.
I bless you for all you support, always.


For the uncompromised word of God imparted into my life I thank
God for his true servants.  Sincere thanks to my pastors and every
spiritual teacher that has made a deposit into my life.

# Creation's Path is…

…A journey through life and all of its experiences.
…A narrow walk in Him of righteousness.
…A choice we all make

## Creation's Path is…

…Knowing who God is
…A journey allowing His word to prevail in all things
…Submission to Him in all things at all times

## Creation's Path is…

…Patience, kindness, goodness, faithfulness
…Love, peace, joy,
…And Rewards in obedience
…Blessings
…Giving

## Creation's Path is…

…Following Him when you don't know what's next
…Trust-in Him above all

## Creation's Path is…

…My life destined to touch yours through a poetic journey of faith.

# Author's Prayer

May this collection of poems encourage your life to…
Live beyond the human eye.
Be led by the Spirit of God.
Trust beyond the doubt and doubters
Believe in Him always
Walk your own journey in Creation's Path.

*"Trust in the Lord with all your heart*
*and lean not on your own understanding; in all your ways*
*acknowledge him, and he will make your paths straight."*

**Proverbs 3:5-6 NIV**

# Table of Contents

Faith in action brings manifestation
Of your victory when you faint not.
Don't give up and always
Trust God's word.

*A journey of faith.*

# Every Time

Every time you see me through
Life's seemingly difficult storms,
I stand in awe of you.
Your mighty hand,
Your power that prevails,
Your amazing grace
That comes upon me to stand
Every time.

*Sharon D. Holliday*

# Faith Triumphs

Faith rises in triumphs
In that moment you
Taste the pleasures of God's promises

Though life challenges your faith,
You're unmovable, steadfast, and abounding,
Stance is the hallmarks of Him in you.

Manifested victories are yours.
Something you would have never known
If you doubted
Gave up
And quit.
Something to remember when you face the next
Test, trial, or temptation.

Faith is something to act on
At all times.
To experience it triumphs
Time and time again.

# Faithful Journey

We endure the storms
With joy and peace
Knowing that
We win.

We stay on the path
That our Creator has
For each of us
For his plan for us is not of evil but a hope and a future.

When we walk as he predestined,
And when we walk by the Spirit of God.
We find Him in every step.

Sharon D. Holliday

*"You will call upon Me and go and pray to Me, and I will listen to you.*
*And you will seek Me and find Me, when you search for Me with all your heart.*
*I will be found by you, says the Lord"*

**Jeremiah 29:12-14**

*Sharon D. Holliday*

# This Time I Laughed!

It happened again!
But this time I laughed.


Like a flood,

     Life changed!

          All the arrows that pointed right reversed.

What happen!
I just don't know
But, this time I laughed!

Why?

Although victory appeared gone,
In my heart I felt this overwhelming presence of

Peace!
Joy!

So, this time
I laughed!

"But thanks be to God, Who in Christ always leads us in triumph...

*[as trophies of Christ's victory]*

...and through us spreads and makes evident the fragrance of the knowledge of God everywhere."

**2 Corinthians 2:14 Amp.**

Sharon D. Holliday

# Life's Rose Petal Storms

Heavy showers
    pour on the
        garden of my heart

My once beautiful petals
    Were exposed ~
        The storms were merciless.

My once admired beauty
    And delicate fragrance appeared gone
        As the darkness
           Covers the light

     ~
You are my Rose of Sharon

     ~
    Morning came
        The sun shone again
           I looked at the light
               As it looked upon me

From a lifeless
Drooping feeble flower
In the storms of life
I cast my cares upon you
My hopes transferred to faith
Head lifting power strengthens me.

     As I rejoice

     My petals unfold
        I am more beautiful than before
        My garden reflects
           Your Glory
        I endure *life's rose petal storms.*

"May the God of hope
fill you with all the joy and the peace
as you trust in Him,
so that you may overflow with hope
by the power of the Holy Spirit."

~ Romans 15:13 ~
NIV

*Sharon D. Holliday*

Without you I am nothing
Without you
I can do nothing.

# I Behold...

...All of who you are.

Today I rose at dawn
and gazed across the lake.
I viewed the beauty of creation.
The sun perfectly shaped
round with a unique color of gold.
Appearing as if it were sitting
On the edge of the water,
Only touchable with the heart.
~God~
Creator of all things.

His work is magnificent,
beyond human ability, beyond our capacity to dream.
I sat and looked at all the things that encompassed me.
I thought of all the things in my life I have seen;
the plants, the trees,
tropical beauty indeed, clear blue and green waters,
mountains seen both far and near,
water falls, gentle rains, animals, and
Mankind-
God's creation of His likeness.
There is nothing that didn't start without Him.
It's hard to imagine the earth without form and void.
Because Your Spirit came moving through
we now behold Creation's Path.

Sharon D. Holliday

# Creation's Path

Transformation by Your spoken Word.
A change instantly made.
You set the course for man to follow.
You gave him complete authority, dominion, and reign
over all your creation.
He gave up his reign when he disobeyed.
But God's love surpassed the sin of man
and restored Creation's Path for man once again to reign.
As the sun rise each day so can we,
beyond the sin, beyond the doubt, beyond the fear, beyond limitations.
As the dawn breaks through the darkness
so does His love and His light penetrate
the darkness, the sins of man and the
doubt that brings unbelief.
Restoration only comes through acceptance of Jesus Christ.
Being clothed with His authority, filled with His Word,
and endowed with His power
man can reign again.
Going forth in the earth with authority, dominion, and reign.
He speaks with authority once more.
Transforming lives and situations
he encounters.
Changed from a state of void and darkness,
man created in the likeness of God
once again on Creation's Path.

# First Love

When the sun sets
and the moon and stars
Light the sky above
Before I close my eyes
I think of You
My first love.

You comfort me.
Your peace over shadows me
As I lie down for the night.
You are the one I whisper
Things before I say good night.

Time travels without intervals.
Another day at its awakening.
The light is appearing,
At lagging speed it seems.
It's dawn!

When I open my eyes
My awareness is of You.
My lips utters.
My first fruit goes to you.
In prayers of admiration and thanksgiving
My heart beats in awe of You in Your presence.
I love You so.

My heart listens for your guidance.
My life is by design.
My day is filled with meditations of You.

Each day begins with
You
And ends with
You Lord.
My first love.

*Sharon D. Holliday*

I see You in color
   The gold that displays the
      Divine nature of who You are
         Magnificent Everlasting Father
I see You in color
   The silver that reveals
      Your wisdom as you speak to my heart
I see You in color
   The white that covers me with peace
      In the time of trouble
The black that mourns
   When I sin
And the red that showers me
   And draws me back in
      With love
I see You in color
   The brown that causes me
      To humble myself
         And submit wholeheartedly unto you
I see You in color
   The amber that burns
      With passion to live out my
         Destiny to the glory of who You are
         God
I see You in color
      The blue that opens the throne room
         As I sup with you in prayer
The lavender that comforts me in sorrow
The rose that reassures me
   That I have my Heavenly Father's
   Care
I see You in color
      The emerald that reminds me that
         You are omnipresent
            You are always there
I see You in color
   The orange that radiates
A heart of praise and joy unspeakable
The teal
   My provider
The turquoise, O healer You are
And  Rainbow
   You are my freedom
      I have a covenant relationship and promises
         For You are faithful
I see You in color
   That color is love that saved me when I was lost.

I see You in color

I found myself
when I found you O Lord,
and submitted
wholeheartedly unto you.
With confidence in you
I am confidently me.
Now to another
I say
"In Him Be…

. . . Confidently You"

# The Human Rainbow

My skin is brown
It's not cursed
It's not something to hold
Me down

My sisters and my brothers
Your shades may be darker
Or lighter than mine
And that's ok

We are all mankind
Our pigmentations aren't meant to
Determine who we are

We are sisters and brothers
Our color brings out the beauty of diversity
We are the human rainbow
You and me
No matter what color that might be

# I'm Not Afraid to Dance

At last
The pain
The sorrow
The things that seems unbearable
Is not the focus of any situation

At last
They are my songs
They are my cheers
And they are my celebrations

At last
When I'm faced with pain
My focus is the strength that I shall gain
Because I've been there before
And I've learned a little more

At last
When the sorrows come
I know they will pass

At last
I can see the warning signs
I can hear the voices of envy and deceit

At last
I can sincerely smile
I can run with confidence
And if anyone or anything rise up to hinder me
I can leap over it like a horse leaps over a hurdle
Because I know that there is a finish line to reach
Where I am already the winner

At last
Before I start anything
I'm not afraid to dance

*I will build you up again and you will be rebuilt, O Virgin Israel.*
*Again you will take up your tambourines and go out to dance with the joyful.*
**Jeremiah 31:4**

*Sharon D. Holliday*

# My Personal Journal

A dance is an expression
For me it is a movement in celebration
Through the many changes and challenges
As I journey through life
We live and we learn
And we can choose to dance

When things happen
Wrong or unjustified
Walk in love in spite of
Do what's right anyway

Another life's lesson learned
Do not worry
Truth and lies can always be seen
By God

If you do as God would do
You can dance

Today I ran into an old friend
That reminded me of my past
I felt sad for just a moment
But I remembered who I am today
So, I introduced myself as if the past no longer existed

I walked away, sanctified from yesterday
So I danced

I put this personal reminder
In my journal each day
No matter what changes, challenges
And things of the past come my way
I remember it's a part of life
Just live and trust in God
And dance.

# When life feels like Job...
## ...Do as he did

Sons and daughters of God
You are
Upright
Righteous in Him
Strives of perfection
Everyday
Seeking My Face
Even when evil comes your way

Sober, vigilant, fully aware
You recognize that satan is there
To sift you like wheat
And bring you defeat

You do not listen
Confessions of faith
I hear you speak

-then~
Off go the Angels
They heard My word
At your command

In a moment's time
To give you a hand
To lift you up
And carry you through

Listen closely
Heaven is cheering for you

You hold fast to your confessions
Your integrity too
"I Am" stands in desire to testify of you
When you do
He loses the shackles
That tries to hold you down
When life feels like Job
"I Am" turn your captivity around.

*Sharon D. Holliday*

# A Journal of Thoughts

We journey through life.
One moment at a time.
And thoughts old and new
Run rapidly through our minds.
Some thoughts
Have made someone rich.
Some thoughts
Have made some man's life better.

This makes me think.
How important are the thoughts we have?
Although, some thoughts.
Are better left unspoken.
Unheard by another's ears.

Our thoughts are
Recorded memories.
Prayers
the spoken word
Are seeds
We are privileged to sow
Time and time again.

Thoughts can
bring us laughter that heals.
Tears,
Encouragement, reminders,
That spurs you to overcome and rise again.
Thoughts have power and they are important.

The greatest thoughts and feelings expressed is
A journal for life itself.
God has thoughts of us that never grow old.
He expresses them in His written Word.
I love knowing
He thinks of you and me
So dear and constantly.

Whenever I experience something,
a thought reminds me,
A journal of His Words,
That are filled with life and power every day.
A journal
Filled with guidance that leads the way.
His word to read each day.

I found myself in a place
I've been before.
Looking for the exit
and there was no door.

I knew I had gotten here
One time too many.
And there must be a way out,
And futuristically returning here
There won't be any.

Just that thought, just knowing some way
Some how gave me the hope.
I needed to find my way.
Right there I meditated on all the things
That ever gave me
Hope for anything.

In the very depth of my heart I could hear
You say, "Don't give up.
This is not where you belong".

Right there is where I gain my strength
And the confidence to stand again.
As you reach out your hand
I heard you say, "you still have me"
Right here
Do not sway.

It's alright.
I am always here
And when things seem the hardest,
That's the place I am the closest.

Just trust in Me,
And when you do
Without looking back.
I'll bring you through.

I know that life,
Has not been easy,
But
Stand in me and you will see.
Be confident and look ahead.
You have not failed, but won instead.

*Don't*
*Give*
*Up*

*Don't*
*Give*
*Up*

*Don't*
*Give*
*Up*

*"For the Lord your God is the one who goes with you*
*to fight for you against your enemies to give you victory."*
**Deuteronomy 20:4**

*Sharon D. Holliday*

# Woman of Strength

The words you speak.
Are words of power.
They are words that build
And make each day a day of hope,
An expectancy of nothing less than God's best.

The words you speak.
Are words of confidence,
In someone greater than yourself;
Transferred to the listener's ear.

The words you speak are words
That infiltrate the heart.
Ones very being,
For they are words of wisdom.

Woman of strength
You are an example to others
Because you live by the words you speak.
The words you speak
Are not your own.
They are the words of our Father.
Spoken to give us faith to endure
Life in all its circumstances.

I value who you are,
I honor you.
Woman of God,
Woman of strength.

*Beyond What You See*

We are all different
But all one in the same.
Some say we are highly complex
And most unpredictable.
We come in all forms,
Tall, short, skinny, or full.

Our hair can be natural, curly, straight,
Permed or weaved.
Our skin is beautiful ebony
Cocoa, butterscotch, or none of these.

We can be
Witty and smart,
Deep or simple.
And maybe not
Or just versed in life's art.

The question is,
Is that all you see?

We can work hard, take care of our children.
Aid our man.
We can stretch a dime,
A dozen times.
But in all of that
What's on the surface is not all of who we are.
Instead of looking at the outward things
Look at the inner me.

In the image of God
He specifically created me
"Woman."
Capable of reflecting His love, truth, strength, goodness,
Wisdom, and His beauty
Beyond what you can see
Is who we are
"Woman."
And only through Him will you really see me.

*Sharon D. Holliday*

Don't be afraid to dream big.
Don't worry if your dreams will come true.
Remember who you are
And who put the dream in you.

Dream Big.
The day will come that it will no longer be a dream
But reality.
Because you weren't afraid to hold to what's inside of you
And reach out to make your dreams come true.

# Dreamers Soar

We are dreamers.
You and I
We have dreams
That seems bigger than the sky.

We see ourselves soaring
Beyond the eye
And when we voice such things,
One may laugh
And another may listen,
But only the one that sees
Can catch such a vision.

We know the dreams
We have are beyond our own capacity.
So we trust the One that
Gave the dreams and
The vision inside of you and I.

Like riders
In a chariot
He guides,
He carries us beyond every obstacle.

We succeed, we reach our destiny
Because
We dare sit and watch passers by.
We dreamers soar
Beyond the sky.

Sharon D. Holliday

Trust in the Lord with all your heart,
And lean not on your own understanding;
In all your ways acknowledge Him,
And He shall direct your paths.

~Proverbs 3: 5-6~
NKJ

Only you O' Lord
Can supply the light we need

You are ...

# ...The Light of Our Paths

# Suits and Skirts

A suit just passed me by.
And another one after that.
The next one that came past was one
With a skirt.
Their hands were both filled.
In one were a briefcase and the other
Was either a cup of coffee or coffee and a purse.

I sat and watched them gather around the table.
And wondered what they were about.
Did these suits and skirts know you?
For their choice of words and laughter
I had my doubts.

Not one reflected you in anyway.
I prayerfully thought I desired that they all know you.
So up I rose just to pass them by and to say.
Hello, "Are you all having a blessed day?"

After getting a cup of coffee
I sat back down
With my coffee and my books.
I hoped to let them know that you were
Hanging around when they would take a look.

But the suits and the skirts continued what
They were doing and more were passing by.
But for your reasons I was lead to do no more.
Lord, what is this and why do you have me here?

The time was near my time to go.
So I gathered my things and
I nodded my head as saying good-bye.
As I passed them
My Bible caught their eye.

One laughed and said, "do you believe what's in that book?"
I shook my head, with a smile and an inviting look.
"Yes" was my reply.
And He said, "one minute please,
I just knew it was something, you sitting there!"

They all pushed their things aside a humbled look in their eyes.
Can you show us God's way, we all have greater needs.
Your plan began to unfold, I just had to obey.
I later then rejoiced because,
The suits and skirts all found you that day.

*Sharon D. Holliday*

# He Waits For You

Born of a virgin,
Destined
Understanding
His purpose.

He lived.
He sat the example
of love beyond us.

He experienced
Rejection.
Sinless yet accused.

No complaint
Crucified and died.
Rose from the grave
Our debt of sin fully paid.

Redeemer
Savior
My Lord
And Intercessor.

King that reigns.
He shall return.

The Way,
The Truth,
And the Light.
The One that gave
His all just for you.
Now
He waits for you.

The way I believe
Is like nothing's impossible
I've come to know who God is
Now, doubt has no more control

My thoughts are no longer my thoughts
They are words of faith
In someone greater than myself "God"
The Creator
The One that said "let there be light"
And it was and still is today

The One that said "Let Us make man"
And He did
In Our image and give him dominion to reign
although through his disobedience
Man gave up his authority
Ah! Satan thought
That was the end for you and me
Loving Father that God is
Made a way to cleanse our sin
Connecting us to Him again

Jesus, God's only begotten Son
Came to seek and save the lost
Shed His blood upon that Cross
Confessions from my mouth
Sinner that I was
I'm no longer lost
Hallelujah! I know
I now reign by the way of the cross
I believe my Redeemer lives
He owns the cattle of a thousand hills
I'm not moved by the circumstance
I dream the impossible dreams
He gave them to me anyway
So I stand in faith as He makes the way
I speak to mountains
I expect them to move
By His words, I proclaim
It is done
In Jesus Name

Some call that crazy faith

Sharon D. Holliday

# Crazy Faith

What I have is not some religious tool
It's the power of God
And I shall not be moved
I believe no weapon formed against me
Shall prosper
I know I am the head and not the tail
Finally my brethren I AM strong
I am strong in the Lord and the power
Of His might
I'm dressed in the whole armor of God.
I keep it on.
I am able to stand against the wiles of the devil
I refuse to wrestle against flesh and blood
I may look foolish in the eyes of the natural man
But in yourself you will never understand

Be not wise in you own eyes
It's the foolish things
He uses to confound the wise
I give and expect the promise of return
Wealth and riches are in my house
I have no need that God can't supply

I know
Crazy faith,

I believe like nothing is impossible
Doubt has no more control
Impractical, senseless-
No,
I'm one of the just
I walk by faith and not by sight
I exercise my faith
Crazy as it seems…
I believe there is nothing
According to His word
By this 'crazy faith you say
That He won't make the way.

LORD, you have assigned me my portion and my cup;
    you have made my lot secure.
The boundary lines have fallen for me in pleasant places;
    surely I have a delightful inheritance.
I will praise the LORD, who counsels me;
    even at night my heart instructs me.
I have set the LORD always before me.
Because He is at my right hand,
    I will not be shaken.
Therefore my heart is glad and my tongue rejoices;
    my body also will rest secure,

v.11

You have made known to me the path of life;
you will fill me with joy in your presence,
with eternal pleasures at your right hand.

Psalm 16: 5-9, 11   NIV


# You Are My Inspiration,

You encourage my soul
and
to You I commit myself
to do Your will O Lord.

Sharon D. Holliday

# A Poem

A canvas of words
A meditation of the heart in its deepest form
A word spoken
A prayer heard and answered.

A voice of truth
A voice of simplicity
A word that captures an emotion, yet,
A word of power that compels you to action.

A poem

A word that creates vision beyond sight
A dance inside
A beautiful ballet
A language used by God to guide our lives.

A poetic heart that hears
And writes

A poem.

# "Write For Me"

Yes, yes! Is my reply.
I want to be your writer Lord
I listen to your voice and at the stroke of the writer's pen
I will share the joys within.
"Write for Me" I heard Him say.
And yes, yes! Will always be my reply.
I want to be your writer Lord
I'll share the gift around the world
from beginning to end.
A soul needs lifting,
a broken heart mended,
dreams restored.
Just speak the words to my heart,
O' Lord inspire my thoughts.
I know
One word from you can transform lives.
Someone dejected hears from You
Can rejoice again.
At that thought alone.
Yes!
I am your writer Lord
I hear your voice and at the stroke of the writer's pen
I can bring Your light to others and unite friends
I can encourage Your love to grow
with this gift you chose to give to me.
Yes, Yes! Lord I want to write for You,
because I Love you so.
~

This request I have of You.
As You have anointed me anoint my readers too
I pray for them to hear Your voice
and for the ones that are lost
for them to be drawn to You .
~

"Write For Me" I heard Him say.

Yes, yes! Is my reply.
As you speak to my heart I will write to uplift
Others to draw them to you.

*Sharon D. Holliday*

# This is My Special Dedication

To My Heavenly Father
Loving you always

# The One Who Gave Me the Gift
# *and*
# Inspires All My Writings

# Your Love Is

Your love is like the rays of sun.
That shines upon my face.
It has the power to change
And brighten my day.

Your love is greater than the joy
That sweet laughter brings;
When someone says,
Those special yet funny things.
Your love is the bonding glue,
That mends my heart when things occur.

When my life seems to be in fragile little parts,
Your love is the foundation,
I build upon each day.
Your love is the key,
The answer to every problem.

LORD,

Your love is what you gave me,
To show me the way.

*Sharon D. Holliday*

Have you not known? Have you not heard? The everlasting God, the Lord, the Creator of the ends of the earth, does not faint or grow weary; there is no searching of His understanding.
He gives power to the faint and weary, and to him who has no might He increases strength [causing it to multiply and making it to abound].

Even youths shall faint and be weary, and [selected] young men shall feebly stumble and fall exhausted;
But those who wait for the Lord [who expect, look for, and hope in Him] shall change and renew their strength and power; they shall lift their wings and mount up [close to God] as eagles [mount up to the sun]; they shall run and not be weary, they shall walk and not faint or become tired.

Isaiah 40: 28-31
AMP

Lord,
The most precious
Moments that life has are...

# ...Times with You.

# *Another Day*

Before the crack of dawn
I'm up again
I'm Thankful

Something new
A day I've never seen
New opportunities awaits

Everything is quiet.

Time to meditate
Read
Listen
And pray

I'm here with you
You are here to guide me through
Another day

*Sharon D. Holliday*

# Waterfalls

Water falls rapidly

Down stream

Off the edges

Into a gentle flow

Creating

A peaceful ambience

*Waterfalls.*

# Enjoying Life

People walking
A smile here and there.
Some sitting,
Relaxing,
Absorbing the serenity
Of all You have given us to enjoy.

There come times in our lives.
That you just have to find a place.
That can bring you
Back to where you
Were meant to be.
Even if it only lasts for a moment.

*This is the day the Lord has made;*
*let us rejoice and be glad in it.*

**Psalm 118:24**

*Sharon D. Holliday*

# Relax In His Goodness!

When I think of His goodness.
I just
Lean back
With a smile and a grin
On my chase,
"My thinking chair" that is.

I am mesmerized.
In Him alone.
And comforted in His love.
All at once
While I relax in His goodness.


*Cast your cares on the Lord*
*and he will sustain you;*
*he will never let the righteous fall.*

**Psalm 55:22**
NIV

# Shut Up

Behind closed doors
I conquer
The real world

You and I
All alone
I meditate
Words of faith
Encouragement
A new song.

Test and trials
Yes they're raging
Like fireworks
Exploding
Vibes of doubt
And unbelief

I STAND
No worry
No need
I confess
I'm His child
The Word
I've learned
In faith
Conquers
Every trial

Years
I've invested
Yes, in me
His word
To stand and maintain
My victory

So in my private quarters
It's You and me
There I pray
I sing
And dance
Cry out
Before it's over
I even shout

You're there
I cast my care
You answer my prayer
Provides my every need
No need to doubt

Time with you I
Shut up
Sup with you
Listen too

This is our time
And when it's time to go
Your presence
Never depart
To your glory
I show
Confidence
Love
Peace
Joy and more
Wherever I go

I
Shut up
With you Lord
That
Through me
You
Others will come
To know

Sharon D. Holliday

Value the people that you encounter.
Value their purpose in your life.
And thank God for allowing them
To be a part of your life
For whatever purpose it is.

# Special People...
# ... Special Purpose

*The Lord reigns, let the earth be glad; let the distant
shores rejoice...For you, O Lord, are the Most High over
all the earth; you are exalted far above all gods.*

**~Psalm 91:1,9~**
(NIV)

# There She Is Again

There she is again.
She may not have all the
Elaborate things that brings
Comfort and joy to me.
But she has something,
No money
Could buy.

She's that ruby in my life.
She's special in ways
No one else can compete.

There she is again.
Girlfriend to the bone,
When I'm going through,
She's there.
Her language is clear.
Her words are comfort and action,
Although her personality is quiet and
She can go un-noticed.
But her voice is loud and clear in just being there.

She prays and believes in her heart.
She studies His word
And lives a life of His Love.
She reminds me of another one so dear,
My Mother-
There she is again-
My sister.

*Sharon D. Holliday*

My grandfather's shoes are old and worn
But not from hard work or the labor of his hands.
My grandfather's shoes are old and worn
From obeying God's command.
You see each day my grandfather rose up early in the morn.
I would peek out my door because I would wonder,
"Where's my grandfather going?"
He never missed a day.

One day my mind told me, go follow him you'll see.
In a whisper,
"Grandfather, may I accompany thee."
My child he said to me "it's yet very early get your rest,
There will be time for you and me.
I have work to do before
Dawn come breaking through"
Trust me child, what I do
Is vital for you."

My grandfather was not very tall
Or big in stature at all
But his integrity stood out
Around my home town.

When people speak of him today
They remember his mule and plow,
His wagon with automobile tires.

Though I did not understand
His early morning plan
Many remember that
He was an extraordinary man.
Holy in his ways,
I remember those days
From that big spiritual book,
The "Bible" that sat upon his lap
In the evenings
he read until he went to bed.

Oh, how he would pray
I believe I am and others too
Are his living victories today
Not of those old and worn shoes
But of the special time he took
To meet his Heavenly Father
In a special place
Before he started the day.

# My Grandfather's Shoes

My grandfather's shoes were old and worn
I value each step he took that got them that way
Because that was the time he took to pray.
I'm sure those prayers kept me through the years
And got me past some of my childhood fears
But more importantly
I'm sure they had something to do with where I am today.
I know his name-his integrity-has helped me along the way
But it was the prayers that kept me until I sincerely found
My Heavenly Father.
I now have my special place
To sit with Him
To talk, to listen, to worship.
I walk in my grandfather's shoes
I take time to pray.

# Real Life, Real People, a Real Friend

I've had people in my life
That was sensitive and caring,
Calculating and cruel;
There have been those that
I hoped in their good deeds to be sincere and honest,
But just in a matter of time
the jealousy
The hate reveal themselves.
You wonder
How could smiles be filled with lies?
truth hidden
and in times
Character's voice
Seems silenced
What a shame that is-
When you give all you can

Life can change in a moment,
Left with nothing it seems
Not as lack.
Just moved, but steadfast and abounding faith~

**"Trusting God-and attending His peace."**

In times like
This where I grasped my soul and commanded it to be still.
And realize that I've been built up.
For such a time as this,
Not to be torn down,
But to be thrust into my own destiny.
Blessed is the **man** who makes the LORD his **trust**

Sharon D. Holliday

I will trust Him always.

How do you trust man? "By faith in God."
No matter what, love.
Remembering Joseph, the dreamer and Jesus too,
All the things they went through.

Love can carry you, but hate
Will stop where you're going.
I'm confident in who I am and my purpose.
In this I find myself understanding personalities,
And the spirit that drives them and how to avoid
The things that cause this kind of grief.
~Prayer~
Keeps me.
I know that there are true, caring, good, and honest people
That have sincere compassion toward others.

They are there, sometimes in distance because, it's where God allows,
Never to look down on you, but to remind you that God is still there.
Love never fails us.

I know people that know what real love is.
I write this to say I'm thankful to God for you listening to Him.
You are always there where He allows you to be near or far
I can always count on your prayer

This is real life, real people
And you are a real friend.
In the image of Him doing
That friendship thing again.

# She's Like Me

She will make you smile
When things are not funny.
Although she is genuine.
You would never discern outwardly
The pains she's going through or has gone through.
She's learned how not to let it show.
She's like me.

She will love you
When you've done her wrong.
And help you if you needed her still.
Cause she's led by the Spirit.
Never selfish revengeful motives.
She's like me.

She puts her heart in all she does.
As she diligently carries out
Domestic pleasures or professional tasks.
She strives to always give her best.
She is known for her spiritual savvy.
Her goals go beyond just passing the test.
She's like me.

She gives you words of wisdom,
That will lift you up
At your lowest point.
In that you can experience her strength.
That only the joy of the Lord gives.

She is earnest,
Even in tough love when it is required.
Tough love is meant to be admired
Not to feel good.
Tough love is truth-not opinion.
She understands
Truth received and acted upon
Produce growth.

She's appealing in dress,
Her taste is exquisite.
She has beauty and poise.
Although sometimes a bit seemingly shy.
Her ambience is tropical,
Exotic, and peaceful.

Who she is,
Is wrapped up in her creator's design.

Whether a friend, mother, daughter, sister or wife.
She's like me
Cause.
Like me
God's Spirit now guides her life.

*Sharon D. Holliday*

# The Holy Spirit

The Holy Spirit comforts us when we need comforting.
Like the arms of a loving mother
That keeps her child secure
And gives him the confidence
That nothing can harm him.

He reminds us of the peace we have that surpasses all understanding
When the storms arise in our lives, trouble on every side,
He brings back the memories of the promises of God.
The Holy Spirit is the source of strength, the power of God through grace
That comes upon us when we feel our journey has been,
Too long, to hard, and want to quit.
He reminds us of the joy we have
Which dries our tears and cause
Us to sing, dance, and rejoice again.

The Holy Spirit draws us to the source of life when we've lost our way.
He draws us back to God and refills us.
He fills the voids in our lives,
In times of loneliness and mourning.
He reminds us of God's love.
He is a stronger shoulder to lean on for support, encouragement, and confidence.

The Holy Spirit warns us of danger ahead.
He guides us to the ways of escape.
To maintain the victories in life
We already have.

The Holy Spirit is our reminding source of confidence,
The victory in every challenge,
The teacher of all things.
He reveals to us what we need to change and shows us how.

The Holy Spirit is as gentle
As the rain that falls as mist,
But more powerful than a raging storm
That tear sails as we journey on.
He is a Gift from God
Our very present help.
The one that leads us in the earth
To accomplish
What God has purposed us.

The Holy Spirit is available to each of
Us as a child of God
For everything.

# *Poetic Journey of Faith Lessons*

"Life can *feel* like a roller coaster up, down, flipping, shaky, and even frightening but the truth of the manner is not to get caught up in unstableness of the emotional zone that life presents. Instead, *trust* God. Allow Him to be the focus in the midst of the joys or the sorrows; the good, the bad, and the ugly, the mountain highs or the valley lows because where He is victory is inevitable."

~

"Walking steadfastly and unmovable in faith will bring you peace that sustain you and illuminate the paths you are destined to take."

~

"In all things give thanks, the right attitude of the heart will make a visual difference and enhance good success"

~

"Giving up what's in your hand at his request can bring forth more than you have"

~

"Knowing Him enlightens, obeying Him is more."

~

"Value people, love them more."

~

God's Plans is always the best plan.

*"Enjoy serving the Lord and he will give you what you want."*

**Psalm 37:4**

*Sharon D. Holliday*

# Give thanks

But thanks be to God! He **gives** us the victory through our Lord Jesus Christ.
1Corinthians 15:57 NIV

The sounds of joy and gladness, the voices of bride and bridegroom,
and the voices of those who bring thank offerings to the house of the LORD,
saying, "**Give thanks** to the LORD Almighty,
for the LORD is good; his love endures forever."
For I will restore the fortunes of the land as they were before,' says the LORD.
Jeremiah 33:11 NIV

In that day you will say: "**Give thanks** to the LORD, call on his name;
make known among the nations what he has done,
and proclaim that his name is exalted.
Isaiah 12:4

**Give thanks** in all circumstances, for this is God's will for you in Christ Jesus.
1 Thessalonians 5:18 NIV

~

God has used my passion to turn my life, giving me something that I love that
brings me joy, gives me satisfaction, while it is an appointment with him to carry
out my assignment, my destined journey with pleasure.
With all His provisions.

# A Destined Journey

I walk a destined journey
Confidently so
'Cause I know
He leads the way
No matter where I go

The vision seems so big
I keep my eyes on Him
So I can clearly see
I must steadfastly walk
He's invested His self in me

Though there does come times
I really don't understand
But I just trust and obey
I honor His command

I walk a destined journey
I'm destined to fulfill His plan
Every provision met
No matter where I go
As I walk this destined journey
His Glory is what I hope to show
And Jesus they come to know

Amazingly enough He chooses
People too
To aid you 'til you're through
And when I bow to thank Him
I thank Him for your faithfulness
For I am grateful 'cause I know
On this destined journey
For me, He sent you

To every person that plays a part of making this journey successful.

Sharon D. Holliday

God so loved the world that He gave His only begotten Son, that whoever believes in Him should not perish but have everlasting life. For God did not send His Son into the world to condemn the world, but that the world might be saved.

~

John3:16-17
NKJ

God gave us His Best…

…Salvation.

# Forecasting

Partly cloudy
Rainy
A storm is headed our way.

People rushing, not prepared.

Forecasting
Sunny
Hot
A time for a fun-filled day.

People packing, preparing.

Forecasting
Things to come,
 Some will be ready,
 Some will not.
People preparing, some are not.

Life's Forecast
Eternally.
Heaven or hell.

People prepare, for both.

*Sharon D. Holliday*

# *Prayer*

Come
Sit
Relax
I am here always.

Meditate my Words.
Ponder them in your heart.
Listen closely,
Fear not,
I am here always.

Speak.
No words from your heart
Are misunderstood.
Cry if you feel like it,
Healing is here.

Speak your heart.
And I will listen.
Ask me in.
I will come.

Talk.
Be yourself.
I know you anyway.

Come, trust me.
Follow my instructions.
I am here always.
Talk to me in
Prayer.

Pray this prayer with me if you sincerely desire a change from darkness to light, from a journey to hell to heaven.

*Dear Lord,*
*I am a sinner. I confess forgive me for all my sins.*
*Come into my life right now and live forever.*
*Fill me with your Spirit and lead me.*
*Help me to remain committed to this new life in you.*
*Connect me with the right church and the right people.*

*In Jesus Name,*
*Amen.*

If you received Jesus Christ as your personal Savior through the salvation prayer, please write to me and I will rejoice with you.

*Sharon D. Holliday*

# About the Author

Sharon D. Holliday is an inspiring and anointed woman of God. She is a woman of the word that loves God very much. She is a woman that has worn many hats personally and professionally.

Along with her husband Minister Ransom D. Holliday she is a minister of the word of God. As the pioneer of her local church's children and youth ministry she has dedicated 14 years of ministry its development and spiritual growth for children, teens, parents, and leadership.

She and her husband have two daughters Monica, Sherisa and one son, Tyshon. A son and daughter-in-law Quincey and Akiah. Their three grandsons: L'Isaiah , Quincey Jr. and Steven adds much inspiration and joys to their life with another on the way this year from the union of their son and wife.

She is a published poet and greeting card writer. God blessed her with a gift to be an inspiration to many. Her writings have been featured in national and international publications.

She admires the strength of her mother and father. The special love that they have given her spurs her to be strong in life and God's love has been her foundation to be a woman of God of great inspiration to others.

**Order Form**

*Please print clearly*

Please send me _____ copies of *Creation's Path* by Sharon D. Holliday

Name _____

Company (if applicable)_____

City _____ State _____ Zip _____

Day phone _____ Evening _____

E-mail _____

Cost: **$10.**⁰⁰

| | |
|---|---|
| Quantity of books | $ _____ |
| Subtotal | $ _____ |
| Sales Tax | |
| NC Residents add 7% | $ _____ |
| Shipping & Handling | $ _____ |
| | $ _____ |
| **Total** | $ _____ |

Please send this coupon and you check or money order to:

**Sharon Holliday**
**P.O. Box 13093**
**Durham, NC 27709**

Payable to: **Sharon Holliday**

Online ordering log on to: www.sharonholliday.org
Also for booking, readings, and other engagements contact by email:
poet@sharonholliday.org

*Thank you for your order. God bless you!*